RESILIENCE
IN
RHYME

GLENANCE GREEN

Dearest Emma Sabella (née),

Inner child. Birthright. Inner energy. InnerG. I am writing to you. I am writing for you. Your healing. My healing. Our healing. I've shielded you in a cloak of protection for many years. Buried you deep in a fortress of my pain and love. Neglected the healing of you for the sake of others. Putting the comfort of others before the healing of you, but I sincerely apologize. I haven't had enough empathy for you, Emma Sabella. At times, I've been downright dismissive. Feeling like you have no right to take up so much space in my world. Your voice isn't the one I've always wanted to hear. It brings me sadness. It triggers my deepest fears. It forces me to confront the pieces of myself that I've distanced myself from that are lost, discarded, abused, exploited, and harmed. With you, I carry so much shame. With you, I carry so much guilt. I hold it all in my womb. The grief. The unresolved trauma. My masculine attributes of survival encase you. For some reason, I am unable to release and let go. I haven't allowed myself to love you deeply enough; and for that, I am truly sorry.

Glenance LaVerne

CONTENTS

A love letter to my future self   1
Armstrong Park   5
Book of Life   7
Burning (Wo)man   9
Can I flex? Can I live?   10
Chakra Energy   12

Dear Uncle James   13
Dragonfly   14
Easily Discarded   17
Energy Vortex   19
Hood Trumpets   20
Hyper-Independence Deconstructed   22

I been that…   25
10 Shots   27
Loyalty   30
Masculinity is to Survival as Femininity is to Rebirth   33
Messiah   36
My Mind   38

Night at the [National Public Housing] Museum   41
Once Upon a Blue Moon   47
Our Blackness is Beautiful   48
Patriotism   50
Rebirth   52
Sexual Healing   53

Sologamy: The Ceremony of Self   56
Spirit Guides   61
The Alliteration of FEAR   63
The Children of Grief   64
The morning after…   66
The Motherland   70

The Mourning   73
The Redwoods   76
The Unprayer   78
To Know One's History   81

Wading   82
We Family   87
Who will cry for the little girl?   90
Winning Battle   92

About Glenance aka Dr. G   95

When the growing pains from my healing become unbearable,
I just write them away.

A LOVE LETTER TO MY FUTURE SELF

Queen,

I don't know what lies ahead but I know that you must trust yourself

Trust your heart
Know that the gold you think you're panning for is encapsulated deep within—you have the key—and the only mining that needs to be done is the minding of your own business, instead of perpetually tending to the mess of others
And oh, what a mess they've made
Let them cry over their own spilled milk
And hire someone else to clean their own neglected houses
Your ancestors were diligent domestic laborers
Paving a path for you to write your own way
They did that
so hopefully you won't have to go through that

Trust your mind
That even as fragile as it can be
It is stronger than you consciously know it to be
Wielding power with nothing but willpower
Through sheer belief that anything is possible
There are enough obstacles that exist outside of your mind
To conquer them, you must remove all barriers that exist within it
Decolonization is a way of life
A perpetual state of being and doing
Constant and deliberate
It requires self-accountability first
To the culpability of harm complicit
in your willingness to participate in the activities of any institution
Always proceed with caution

Trust your ordered steps, making moves straight from the
directives of your soul
Tied in knotless braids and inextricably linked to the Universe
Trust the values that ground you in character no matter what
stage you're on
Having a Verzuz battle with personality
You will get knocked down
and you will dust yourself off and try again
Like Ali and Aaliyah

Goddess, you're onto something big
I can feel it
Energetically flowing through our chakras
I can hear it
Whistling to our core while in nature in the wind
I'm meditating on it
I'm preparing for it
I've gathered all of the tools I think you'll need but it will require
you to do the rest

Lean into your magic
Your ability to reinvent and reimagine yourself outside of the
present moment
Your willingness to not let your past define but shape you in
appreciation of Sankofa

Follow your spirit guides
The ancestors who watched over us
Long before the colonizer's religion was ever given to our
people

Teach others how to treat you by demonstrating how well you
treat yourself

Treat others how you want to be treated
Considered and handled with care

Dream big!
Speak life!
Manifest!
Do you!
Reign with freedom and liberation
as you have in every lifetime before this one
An architect of liberation

After all, karmically, it is what you've always been destined to be

With love and supreme benevolence,

Signed...me

Aging like fine wine, I only get mo' betta
Releasing the weight that holds me down

ARMSTRONG PARK

Some say you can't see stars in the city, but I disagree
We just don't look up enough
Hard enough
Long enough

I'm sitting on a hill in Armstrong Park on 44th and St. Lawrence
and just counted at least seven in the sky

The soundscape to my left
Teenage boys on the basketball court nearby, shit-talking one
another with Black boy joy
All smiles

The soundscape to my right
The oldheads lined along the sidewalk in their folding lawn
chairs facing the street with their cargo van doors wide open
blasting Bobby "Blue" Bland and James Brown, making special
requests to a woman named Monique who is DJ'ing their
YouTube station
Big laughter

It's no longer Summertime Chi
but a 70-degree day in November warrants some outdoor
attention
Shorties running free in the outfield of the baseball field
Their childish giggling makes me giggle

30 and 40-somethings jogging around the track for evening
exercise
Everyone in their own zone yet joyfully acknowledging one
another as they make their rounds

The sun sets in the distance behind the tallest building that I can
see
Provident Hospital of Cook County

I'm present
Here with my people
None of whom I know
Yet there is peace
And it is beautiful
Nothing matters beyond this moment
In this moment, we all are choosing to live

In this moment
Together
In peace

When the reddish amber color serving as the backdrop to the horizon of the buildings from the residue of the sun fades to black, I know it's time for me to get up and walk home

For now, I'm present

BOOK OF LIFE

Shedding chapters
Everybody can't go with you

Closed books
Leaving behind the read lines in between

Untold stories
Stuck in the shadow work of my vulnerabilities
Hov said you can't heal what you don't reveal

444
My spirit guides sending angels that's saying baby girl, keep it real

Cataloging the dialogues that weigh heavy on my heart and mind
Archiving the content of life experiences that gives me what feels like an extra lifeline over time

My life
A reference
Unable to be checked out

A rare find
Upon request, behind the front desk of only a few libraries

I've put myself on hold
My call number always available to those who truly need me

I vibe high
Currently in low circulation though

You'd have to know what you're searching for in yourself to find and appreciate the density of what my pages can offer

I am well read

From cover to cover

I've been around the world
and I, I, I have been seen by plenty
Touched and held by many
But few who really understood what a gift they had being
bundled next to a bound me

Yet here I am
Glowing from up high, somewhere deep in the stacks
What was will no longer be
The price just went up
and I am priceless
Step stools and ladders are now required for complete access to
me

Top shelf
You have to level up to touch the sky

The message
The story
The joy
The lesson
Are all still here

As a memory
In the mind

Did you take the time to read me?

BURNING (WO)MAN

Picking up all of these peas in the pot
I'm a poet
You know it
I can't ever stop

My pitch a cappella
No beat here to drop
Became unemployed to come out the box

Mind like a dolphin
My tongue like a fox
I'm keeping it cool
Kelela with locs

If you making history
Come and come work with me
Building community
Like open heart surgery

Breathe

We take anesthesia to just numb the pain
Cut it wide open
Repair from the frame
The roots from the Chi
The system's the same
We can't let us die
A slow death in vain

What is your legacy?
Listen to Ledisi
Everything changes
How do you want to lead?

CAN I FLEX? CAN I LIVE?

We don't want to be capitalists but sometimes we just want some
shit
We came from nothing
Still singing Drake's
Started from the bottom
now we're here
For some of us, that's still at the bottom

We know that capitalism works against us
That it's inextricably linked to the exploitation of Black and
brown bodies
We know it is rooted in anti-blackness
We know that wealth has been colonized and the lens through
which we understand money is inherently flawed
We want people in office who care
We want to believe that the system can work to our advantage
by allowing us to put someone in office who is a candidate of
the people
Some of us want to uplift the values of socialism and have a
productive conversation about what that might mean for our life
chances without it ignorantly being mistaken for and simply
dismissed as communism

We want racial equity
We want healthcare for all
We want to earn a livable wage
and not have to sell every hour of our day to someone else in
exchange for doing so
We want affordable housing
We want access to high-quality public education
We want humanity in the workforce
We want to build businesses in our community
and own homes for our families to inherit so they don't have to
struggle the way we did just to make rent
We want to own land and build community gardens

Not because we feel that we, or anyone for that matter, should own land because it belongs to the Earth
But dammit, if other people are owning everything around us, we want to buy back a little piece of the block for our own too

We want to be down for the cause
but level up on our sneaker game with shoes we can't afford
We want to buy some flashy jewelry
And a few wigs
And a new car
And fresh full sets every two to three weeks without having to do the cheaper fill
And a whole bunch of unnecessary shit we don't really need but like to look at simply because we can

We want to take a few trips around the world with money to blow
And return home to keep fighting the good fight
With our people
For our people
We don't want to bypass opportunities to have a seat at the table
Because we know our values are going to be criticized by those who weren't invited into the room in the first place
For all of the criticism that we do of our own, we know there's still a deck of undealt cards on the table
In many ways, we're still Spike Lee's Jigaboos and Wannabes despite our School Daze being over
All because we dare to want something just for us

Sometimes we just want some shit

Some shit just for us

CHAKRA ENERGY

I suffer from chronic lower back and hip pain like I'm somebody's grandmother, but I know that's where all of the energy from my childhood trauma is stored. My hips valiantly hold my years of shame and unworthiness. My ass, my most prized aesthetic possession, holds the suppression of my anger and rage. My sacral and root chakras are screaming at me. They are blocked and displeased. I am tight, and it feels like I get tighter instead of lighter every year. Lately, I've been loosening my hip flexors and experiencing a rush of emotions thereafter. Whatever I have pushed down is coming back up, and it's calling me to face it head-on.

DEAR UNCLE JAMES

Dear Uncle James,

Thank you for paving the way! For showing our people that Black intellectualism doesn't have to represent the elitism of white structures and racialized practices. But that it can and should be used as a tool to challenge what has been presented to us. To leverage our education, literary consciousness, and lived experiences to engage in truth-telling. Thank you for demonstrating that no matter the time and place, there is always space for us to be ourselves! For reminding us that teachable moments don't have a face.

Thank you for inviting us into *Giovanni's Room* where we used your voice to *Go Tell It on the Mountain* to get free through that which you had to conceal in America yet still chose to live out loud. *If Beale Street Could Talk*, she would sing sweet words of gratitude manifesting as *Notes of a Native Son* in *Another Country* within our own where *Nobody Knows My Name* and there's *No Name in the Street*, not even in familiar company under the light of the lamp post *Just Above My Head*. Thank you for bearing the *Cross of Redemption* and encouraging us to stand tall amid adversity, as you remind us that we are not their negros.

Thank you for reminding us that we are our own!

In solidarity,

Glenance aka Dr. G

DRAGONFLY

Dare I be beautiful? My strange attraction to odd things led me to purchase a necklace made of restored metals. This time at the 57th Street Art Fair. The image? A dragonfly, etched with immaculate imperfections.

Realizing that I'm going through some changes, she represents transformation. The ability to adapt. The willingness to self-actualize. Maturity. Understanding. Evolution. Mentally and emotionally.

An incredible symbol of where I am, where I have arrived. A reminder of what I've been and who I can be.

Good fortune and well wishes. To some, the dragonfly represents prosperity.

On a recent hike through the Franklin Mountains in El Paso, Texas, I saw a dragonfly. Fluttering through the sky. There it was. The second dragonfly in just a couple of weeks.

Nothing major or fantastical happened in real time but spiritually, it did. A deeper connection. An unlocking of another door. A new vision of love.

Freedom. A reconnection with the laws of the Universe. An awareness of the laws of the spirit.

Laws not intended for policing and surveillance but designed for us all to be our greatest selves. One of my biggest flaws is my irritation with others for their lack of desire to not live and do according to their highest good. Regardless of whether it's taught, it lives within us. There is the Law of Choice, yet we still choose chaos...again and again. I guess to some extent, I'm guilty of it as well. Grace.

You only get one shot in this form. My thought is, why not do it right? To grow is to learn the lessons from all of life's many teachers…and do and be better. I am grateful for the dragonfly. As hard as it has been lately, she affirmed that I am well on my way.

*Pay close attention to the spiritual symbols and creatures that the Universe attracts you to. They might mean nothing to others but they definitely mean something **for** you.*

EASILY DISCARDED

I've always been someone who has been easily discarded
Thrown by the wayside
The shadows of my sadness riding the low tide like a plastic straw floating along the shore of the ocean
Making its way to a life source until I am eaten whole
But little do they know, I am plastic
Built to last, so that when I am swallowed by a predator and hit the back of their throat they will choke on me as I devour them from the inside out
Making them scream the Lord's name as they pray that this prey spares them today despite their karma pulling up a front-row seat to watch them reap what they have sown

I am easily discarded
Yet forgiving, so I let it go

And just like that, with a simple disagreement or moment in time, years upon years can go to waste as I am eliminated from the body

I am prey again, released back into the ocean from an asshole who confused submission with loyalty

I float again, on the conditional waves of our collective existence pushing me back to the place where I started

The journey amounted to nothing

When the water settles, I find myself gathered with others who have also been discarded, improperly placed, and handled with a lack of care

We cry together, but our tears are camouflaged by the open waters washing over our faces as our bodies perpetually spin

We are all plastic objects, desperately in search of a home because the homes we once knew couldn't even appreciate us enough to recycle

What we called home wouldn't even bother to see the beauty in our ever-evolving form
Judged by who we are and aren't in one moment in time

Easily discarded
Me and my band of junkies unite along the shore as one united front and push west, with a vengeance
Although all of us won't make it out to the middle of the open waters where we float freely, some of us will

And though we are forgiving, we will never forget

With every new predator that comes our way, we will show them how much we remember as we annihilate them one by one

One chomp on our bodies at a time
Neglectfully destroying the ecosystem of marine life
We don't care
Because no one cared enough about us to not have us out here living raggedy in search of a new home

They only cared for themselves in that one moment in time

And now that one moment in time for them has resulted in the reduction of time for everyone

Discarded

ENERGY VORTEX
– MOUNT LONGONOT, KENYA

This place
Calls out to me
For me

I can feel the vibrations of its magnetic force field
Reverberating through my morsel
Clearing chakras in my torso
Harvested for clean energy

This place heals
Restores
Is a crater
A sleeping stratovolcano
Seeping steam from her pockets

The ground is hot
My guide says it's from the sun
But I felt a small wind tunnel of warmth
Where the sun wasn't shining
Nearly cruising altitude above sea level

You are a vortex of magical energy
And you are absolutely beautiful

HOOD TRUMPETS

Standing on dry grounds with fertile roots that cannot grow
No matter how much it rains, the foliage carries low
Just blocks from Freedom Square at Homan, just so you know

Forced to square up for our freedom, our village pays the toll
In blood, sweat, and tears
In exchange, social control

Hollow bodies hit the grounds with the Sounds of Blackness
Optimistic, making rounds in the midst of madness
As long as you keep your head to the sky, you got this
You can win
And can't nobody tell us what is best
Keep going in
Revolutionize your reformist request
Conquerin'
Pick up a book and go learn a lesson and plug it into the streets
that's missing you as a blessin'

I've been stressin'
Bout how to make abolition the manifestation of a solution
For those who really care, they'll listen with resolution
See no words feel quite right for this moment
We in the midst of an uprising for equity with COVID mask-
free breathin' up on it

Yet I keep pushin'
In the belief there's something better we're cookin'
So please go mobilize your networks instead of just lookin'
From the sidelines of your social media feed
Organizing can't be done from the bleachers, you got to lead
Money, time, and talent
One of three can feel a need
Please proceed

And there's no ideal vision of perfection
If I may make a suggestion, get in where you fit in before the
next election
Make a connection
So we can all start to build to where we're destined

HYPER-INDEPENDENCE DECONSTRUCTED

Hyper-independence
It is a myth
One with real social and material responsibilities forced upon
Black women with long-term consequences that leave us
yearning and desiring to be cared for

My needs are changing
Or maybe I'm just coming into full and complete understanding
of them
I've spent my entire life looking out for myself and those around
me
Having to put on my big girl panties and woman up
Having my own back when things get tough
Having to constantly fight for myself and others
Not being able to depend on many people for my core needs
And for a while that was OK
At least I thought it was

I wasn't making an effort to be like this, I was bred this way
My hyper-independent behaviors had become so
commonplace that I convinced myself that I didn't need
anyone
That I *wanted* people around but didn't *need* anyone
Those around me felt that way too
Especially romantic partners
But I didn't know how to undo this "thing"
How to become less independent
Or if that's something that I even wanted for myself
Partially because I have yet to see one example of a model
partnership arrangement that I desire for myself

I have no desire to be domesticated
Or a full-time stay-at-home mother
Or have to give up my career or the businesses that I run in
exchange for love with material benefits

Or have to compromise things that are most important to me just to say I'm someone's wife
Mad respect to the strong independent women who can and do
I just know myself and I wouldn't be happy
I would constantly feel like something's missing
Like I'm sacrificing key pieces of myself for someone else's liberation when I believe that we can both be free
...together

Nevertheless, my needs are changing
And have been for years
Although I enjoy being independent, I've released my need to be independent and independently take care of any and everything all of the time
As a result of healing and growth, I no longer feel that I have to be independently responsible for everything and everyone important to me

I want to feel protected
I mean, really protected
I want to be able to rely on others for protection
The kind of protection that checks in to make sure that I am of whole mind, body, and spirit
The kind of protection that wraps me in their arms after a hard, long, or bad day just to make me feel alright
The kind of protection that helps further heal the parts of myself that make me feel that I cannot depend on anyone but myself

The kind of protection that makes me feel safe
The kind of protection that gives me comfort and a deeper sense of security
Supporting the healing of my deeply rooted safety trauma

My needs are changing
I need to feel safe
I need to feel protected
I need to feel cared for

I need the help of others to get there

I BEEN THAT...

I been that nigga
From project to project
From public to private

I been that leader
From most loved to most hated
Fuck it, I'm self-celebrated

I been that simp
From doing too little to doing too much
Yet checking my mirror saying you ain't doing enough

I been this raw
From pantry boxed milk, blocked cheese, and mashed potatoes
From Medicaid glasses on picture day, please catch my angle

Been had an attitude
From popping off in these streets to popping into myself for
better health
The residue of old toxic energy saying but you can still catch
these hands

I been this wise
But never a clown for these pennies
I'm counting lives
I been my own savior ever since my Jesus died
From passing the GED at 12 to surviving 12 plus 12 to
graduation for my PhD

Cause I been ambitious, baby
Come look in my eyes
They do stay on the prize

And when I blink just a little
I manifest yet another drive

Surprise
Oop, I think your mockery just made me giggle
Your jealousy kinda of trash, it might just make me wiggle
Like kids watching them toons with jingles that match the riddles

I been that mother
Rebirthing grown lost sons and lonely daughters
Evolving the village exhausted from the sins of our fathers
Generational trauma masked as demeanor unbothered

I been that nigga.

10 SHOTS

10 shots fired on my block in Bronzeville last night.
A shootout.
Near the house. Three from the sender.
Seven from the receiver.
I had just come home within the hour. Someone had taken my spot out front, so I parked in the back.
I was sitting on the couch in my living room when I heard them.
I turned off the light, hit the floor, and crawled over to the front window.
I could hear the commotion from various voices on the street.
"Watch out!"
"Watch out!"
"Aye, check it out!"
"Go through the alley!"
"We on they ass. I was blowin' this bitch."
"Go in the gate!"
"I don't give a fuck. Where's the gate?"
"Let's go! Let's go...NOW!"
"Go in the house! Go in the house!"
"Somebody tried to pull up shootin'."
"Get the fuck in the house!"
"Come on, let's go!"
"Girl, they pullin' up shootin' at people."
"You good?"
"Yea, I just came out my shoes man."

Peeking out, I watched a young man and woman perched down under my porch, hiding for cover.
Heads bobbing up in the direction of the initial shots to see whether it was safe to leave.
I sat kneeled against the wall under my window, also waiting for the chaos to settle.
Hoping that the car that just swerved off into the distance doesn't bend the corner and come back around to start shooting at the bodies crouched down between cars, running down the

street, or temporarily nesting under and near my house.

My anxiety clenching the heart in my chest.
Awaiting a safe moment to step outside to see if everything is OK, if everybody is OK.
My breathing belabored as my mind catches up to my body.
My internal response mechanisms firing off as if I'm out on the street in the midst of the action.

Post-traumatic stress disorder kicking in, harder than the sativa-dominant edible that I had to enjoy my Sunday evening.
Not certain whether the physiological response is being amplified as a result.
My safety-related trauma triggered, once again.
I sit still for a while wondering if anyone is hurt, injured, or dead.
Waiting for the silence.
To cut through the tension.

I called a couple of loved ones.
To inform someone that I was home alone.
No answer.
Just me and the neighbors who text.
When it was over, everyone went on their way.
I stepped outside momentarily and resumed my place on the couch.
Adrenaline flooding my body.
The wounded child in me still contorted underneath the front window.

The block, resuming to its quiet and perceivably peaceful state of discord.
Just as it did after the drive-by shooting on the block a couple of months ago back in March.
Alone, my mind and body being forced to respond the same.
I couldn't help but wonder how many of my neighbors' bodies feel like they are constantly and perpetually being prepared for and responding to war.

A conversation we never have with one another because things are the way they are, and we've grown accustomed to adapting.

Accustomed to city living.
We simply tell others that we're glad that they're safe and go about our way.
Not thinking twice about the accumulating traumatic microaggressions collecting both in our psyche and souls.

Summertime Chi.
A storm is brewing...
And it has nothing to do with the weather.

LOYALTY

For years, I hurt
Because my loyalty wouldn't let me write this piece
I didn't want to expose what I was trying to protect
So what I refused to reveal went unhealed
But I'm tired of hitting this same wall
Bashing myself in like an aluminum can
Contorted into a fold until I can no longer move

We protect men
Men who lie
Men who cheat
Men who betray our trust
Men who abuse us
Verbally
Physically
Mentally
Spiritually

We protect men
Those undeserving of our love
Those unworthy of our attention
Those exploiting the mastermind of our intellect and savviness

I protected men
Men who did not love me tenderly
Or care for me properly
Those who took what they needed and discarded the rest
Men who mistook my heart for putty and misused it to build a
stronger foundation of walls of protection for themselves and
other women

I protected men
To no avail
To my disadvantage
To not be chastised about not giving a nigga a chance

Or having standards too high for requesting that he come to the table with something substantive to offer
As if a few bills, some pocket change, and good dick are adequate for the stimulation of my heart, mind, and soul

I don't require emotions for a good fuck of the body
Detached like a retina, I can't even see beyond the moment if you have nothing more to contribute

Yet I protected men
In an effort to not be perceived as a man-eating, male-hating, male-basher

Because I love Black men
Deeply
And in my deep love for Black men
My unyielding loyalty
I passively consented to being tortured
Mentally
Emotionally
My mental wellness at stake
Gaslit into thinking something was wrong with me for speaking on what I often observed with my own eyes and felt within my own spirit

Perhaps I made it up
Maybe I'm overthinking
Mayhaps I'm being too hard on him or not understanding enough or not quite hearing what he has to say even though he's repeated it six times as he rehearsed to himself in the car before seeing me and it's still not making a lick of sense

I'm now offended and insulted
Perhaps he's a muthafuckin' pathological liar unworthy of my trust
Daddy issues
Triggered

I didn't want to write this
My loyalty is feeling shame
But the more I hold onto it, the more disloyal I am to myself

Martyrdom
Becoming small so others around me can feel big

Martyrdom
Coating masculinity with femininity to be more digestible to men...and sadly, other women
Despite their loyalty to the toxic hypermasculinity of men
Oop!
I will no longer be disloyal to myself
For the comfort of others

This

Stops

Here

I will protect those who demonstrate care and consideration for others

My loyalty is now reserved for the men and women who want to love with their whole selves, and are not afraid to be loved in return

MASCULINITY IS TO SURVIVAL AS FEMININITY IS TO REBIRTH

I have always best understood my femininity through a masculine lens of social construction. As strange as it may sound, I discovered the essence of my femininity through masculinity and the essence therein through tactics of survival. For a long time, survival felt inherently masculine. I watched the beautifully feminine expressions of my mother's character often go unnoticed and be abused and recycled into a vicious cycle of violence perpetuated by my father when he was around. I often felt that her femininity would be the death of her, not understanding that it was his hypermasculinity that was toxic and non-conducive to survival. Yet and still, growing up, the concept of being feminine or femininity felt pretty foreign to me. I was a tomboy which, according to the dictionary, is a girl who enjoys rough, noisy activities traditionally associated with boys. For me, I was just living and moving in my skin. In my single-parent household of mostly boys, spearheaded by a matriarch, gender roles were turned on its head for all occasions, except for the church. Apparently, Jesus needed to save my soul in frilly dresses and nude pantyhose.

Nevertheless, I obliged. Straddling the fence of every Jesus who wanted to save me for the next 20+ years long before waking up in the decade of 30, I associated the discarded parts of myself as passively femme, punishing almost every man I've ever been with for not loving me the way I wanted to be loved. Whether it was responding with an attitude or changes in my temper, my emotions fled across a sliding scale of conditionality. I'll love you more if you just love me, screamed the little girl inside who never got to be a girl because she was raped into survival on more than one occasion. Being more of a girl meant being less protected from the world. Building walls of protection around my heart with Legos yet I had the audacity to get upset when someone played me like a toy. *You will never love me as much as I love you.* I affirmed an energy that did not necessarily have to be true but it was what I believed because I knew no other experience from a man but to love that which could never truly love me in return. I used to shrug my shoulders and say I didn't care but I did, and I still do. My ex once told me that I had a problem with men. Belligerently, I told him that I did not. But, I did. Every unresolved issue I ever had, I made it their problem. I held them accountable to the expectations that I created in my head. They didn't have to be agreed upon. It was enough that I, clearly the brilliantly superior one, developed them. I shamed them, every time they failed. And when they failed, I felt my own failure. *You hurt me. You're just like my father. Abandoning me. Disliking me.* Hating what he created. I never became the boy that my father always insisted he wished I were. But, I became the masculine girl not emotionally sensitive enough for the boys. A damsel with no patience for the distress, even for distress engineered by my own doing. Covered in laughter as a coping mechanism for my pain, my layers are peeling.

Just a tad beneath the surface of that first ring, I am a masochist. I still refuse to believe I am but my behavior would beg to differ. I desire and attract that which I seek to disrupt. In some strange way, I enjoy that which is emotionally unavailable to me. I crave it. I need it. I understand it. And when it disappoints, as it always does, I feel like someone has done me wrong for not being more than the energy that I both attracted and perpetuated by participation. They say you don't attract what you want, you attract what you are. I'm just like my father. I will abandon you emotionally if you don't give me what I need to connect. I will dislike you if you disappoint me one too many times. And you won't get anything out of me depending on how you choose to engage with me.

This was made abundantly clear when I met her. Her personality, a classic reflection of my own yet manifested very differently. She projected, a lot. Emotions. Unresolved issues.

Triggers that I "triggered" that had nothing to do with me and lived far away from my awareness or stream of consciousness. Apparently, I didn't know how to treat women either, according to her whines and erratic responses alluding to me not treating her how she wanted to be treated. False expectations commenced despite me having no desire to acquiesce. Yet there I was, sitting in my living room being yelled at from the top of her lungs about how hurtful and insensitive I was for not seeing her how she wanted to be seen. And this went on, for months. Late-night calls. Drunk texts. "You don't care about me at all. You're abusive for your silence," I was told after choosing not to respond to what I perceived to be immaturity and ignorance. My long sighs amounted to nothing more than aggravation. Is this how others felt about me?

Truth be told, I did like her. Just not as much as she claimed to have "loved" me. I briefly entertained the thought of going on a journey with her but the evolution of my queerness felt closeted to her and therefore was often not respected. If only I could be disillusioned by my own discomfort. What's now her truth filled with excess baggage is nothing more than a memory to me. But strangely enough, after all these years, it took me opening up my heart to a woman to empathize with every man who's ever loved me deep. Hmph. Mirrors. Masculinity is to survival as femininity is to rebirth.

MESSIAH

Many do not believe in God, yet they seek a Messiah

Something or someone to save them

If Christ, or any other prophet for that matter, were to return for the second coming or the rapture, our level of skepticism masked in intellect for ourselves and one another would prevent us from following

They would need to prove themselves worthy of our loyalty and commitment

Yet, day after day, many of us do not prove ourselves to be loyal and fully committed to much of anything, including ourselves

So... save yourself!

You were gonna be left behind anyway.

She's awakening...inside of me...all on her own
Who am I to be free?

MY MIND

I do want
I do want
I do want
My name is Mind and I do what I want

My mind
Moves so fast, it could bend time
Reorienting itself like fidgeting lug nuts spinning on a wheel
It's always in motion
Calibrating sickness by my ability to get out of bed and show up
for work in the morning
It puts itself on autopilot
Flying through the clouds disappearing into space until someone
says, Good morning!
Triggering its signal to land because my body sits in plain sight
and there's no runway to run away from all of the air traffic it's
forced to control

My mind
Protects itself by deflecting
Ricocheting negativity with a mirror in hand facing you
She is bulletproof
You cannot break her with manipulation
You won't force her to internalize and own what she didn't buy
or reap what she didn't sow
My mind has a mind of its own
Supporting itself by whispering words of affirmation to stay
motivated through the day so if no one else tells it how
wonderful it is, it will still know that it's OK
Kissing its membrane regularly
So it knows what love should feel like when it exists outside of
the mind
Programs codes for hugs on arrival so my body can feel safe in
intimate spaces with strangers around
Lo-fi beats calm its cranial nerves

My mind
Is a powerful thing
So much so, I can't always trust it to have my back because it's always looking out for itself
My mind don't give a damn about what this body doesn't want to do
If it decides that we're going to do something, we're going to do that something
At times, it can be indignant and resolute, thinking that it knows what's best
After all, even if my heart stops beating, this body will live on if my mind keeps breathing

My mind
Is a cocky muthafucka
You can't tell it nothing
It lives in a fortress of confidence made with steel not acquired by mining for coal

My mind is beautiful
Programmed for safety
I have to be careful not to overload it with tasks non-conducive to restoration
One likely coping mechanism of entities as such can be to self-destruct
Program self-destructing in 5-4-3-2...
For now, it's constantly reprogramming itself for wellness whenever I take a seat and simply do nothing
Do nothing?
Do nothing!

My mind
Is precious

My mind
Is subject to change course in the middle of a sentence, both in conversation and on paper

My mind
Is fragile
I should do a better job of taking care of it

I do want
I do want
I do want
My name is Mind and I do what I want

NIGHT AT THE [NATIONAL PUBLIC HOUSING] MUSEUM

Chicago United for Equity After Hours: Telling Chicago's Stories
January 15, 2020

27 years ago, I laid flat on my back
27 years ago, I laid flat on my back staring at the fissured squares
glaring back at me from the ceiling
On a metal framed cot
With just enough cushioning to call it a bed
My mother
My sister
My three brothers nearby
The year was 1993
I was six going on seven
The Housing and Community Act of 1992
Moving to Opportunity for Fair Housing
Hope VI authorizing the demolition of public housing
New stipulations for Housing Choice Vouchers
All in effect

This was our second shelter
But it would not be the last
The first
We were turned away because of capacity
There simply were not enough beds to accommodate my single
mother and her five children
We were there because of domestic violence

The shelter
Just a few beds away from a street corner
Was a safe haven
From my father's fist
And the dark side of homelessness

In 1994, we moved into a house
One that accepted my mother's Section 8 voucher
One that we would not have been able to afford without it
Not like the house we left behind on Bronson when my mother,
with all of her bravery, finally had the courage to leave
Not like the housing development that we left behind a while
back in my hometown of Benton Harbor, Michigan
The complex where we all lived
My grandmother
My auntie
My cousins
Family friends
Hull's Terra was community
And we would soon create another
Apart from family
One where the sight of men's shoes raised red flags about the
tune of your blues that would quickly get your amp disconnected
There could be no adult males in the house
Even if they were the father
Divide and conquer
State-sponsored

One where a failed inspection plus a slum lord could result in
you being rolled right back into rotation
One where we had to check in regularly like we were on
probation
We weren't
We just needed affordable housing
And any changes in our income would impact the delivery of
service
Resulting in potential increases in family contributions to rent
paid out-of-pocket
Criminal convictions of tenants warranted termination, even
those involving youth under the age of 18
Even if that means disowning or separating yourself from your
children
Divide and conquer

State-sponsored

This was the community of Section 8
The community of Housing Choice Vouchers
When I was little, there used to be a gate in the park of the public
housing development where we lived, LaSalle Park Homes
Just a gate
With a latch
One lonely wooden gate in the middle of the park
With a thin slab of wood attached to the bottom for small
children to stand on
And the gate would swing
And swing
And swing around and round
Like a bootleg merry-go-round
Whenever my siblings and I got close, my mother would say
"Get on that gate if you want to and Imma get into that ass"
[Ha. Black mamas.]

She believed that swinging on the gate in the park would
translate to swinging on doors in our house
You see, we only observed these little gates at parks within or
near public housing developments
My mother believed the gate was the root of a systemic problem
not a symptom
She believed that they were placed there intentionally
For little Black kids to swing on
To subconsciously train them to "tear shit up", in her words
And there would be no tearing of shit up in my mother's house
Yet this was the community of public housing

Nevertheless, we created our own community
Of loyalty
Of support
Of protection, that didn't require the involvement of disruptive
external forces
And never did I imagine that 14 years later from 1994 in the

height of the recession of 2008, I would be sitting right here in this neighborhood talking to former residents and members of the Local Advisory Council of the ABLA Homes
Interviewing them about their lived experiences, strikingly similar to my own

One of the first three housing projects in the city of Chicago
Jane Addams Homes
Morphed
Robert Brooks Homes
Morphed
Loomis Courts
Morphed
Grace Abbott Homes
The evolution of ALBA
Addams
Brooks
Loomis
Abbott

The last standing relic boarded up at 1322 W Taylor
They lived at
1263 W Hastings
1510 W 14th Place
1536 W 13th Street
1440 W 14th Street
1410 W 14th Street
Many addresses that you can no longer even pin on a map
At the time, I was a budding researcher
With only one year of professional research experience under my belt
A fellow for Loyola University Chicago's Center for Urban Research and Learning
Conducting an ethnography
Through the oral histories of folks who lived there between 1938 and 2002
I was tasked to a special project that summer

Gathering data, narratives, and stories that could help make the case for a proposed National Public Housing Museum come to life
Reporting the relevance of erecting a relic with historical significance so that people truly understand the importance of such a monument
And the impact that public housing has had on the community
In my research that year
I pondered many things
The gradual deterioration of public housing as it evolved from immigrants white on arrival to primarily people of color

The long-standing negligence of the Chicago Housing Authority or CHA in its administrative responsibilities to the maintenance and upkeep of public housing projects
The invitation of crimes of opportunity as a result of that negligence
The contributions of crack cocaine to the division and
disconnection between Baby Boomers, Gen X'ers, and Gen Y aka Millennials in the Black community
And in my research that year
I learned many things
I had the pleasure and honor of meeting and interviewing the heartbeat of the ABLA community
The late great Commissioner and Founding Chair of this museum Deverra Beverly, aka Miss. ABLA to those who knew her well
I learned things that I had not known in all of my years of being impacted by public housing
Like just how important Local Advisory Councils were and are to the stability of a public housing community

And even in 2008, when the city wasn't funding LAC programs at ABLA, they still managed to supply WIC coupons, bus passes, school supports for young mothers, assistance with getting folks lease compliant, helping folks with utilities and finances, and housing assistance

Because that is what community looked like to them
People looked out for one another
Cared for other people's children
Their time
Voluntarily
For 10, 20-something years
Because they knew that we, as a community, are all that we got
Many of the residents had lived in this community for over 40,
50, 60 years before being interviewed that summer
Some were even the first to occupy their units at ABLA over
half a century ago
Few outside of this community even knew their names
Yet and still, this is for them

LaVert Beverly
Mark York
Betty Houston
Jacqueline Pettiford
Carl James
Deverra Beverly
And countless others
Because without their work
And contributions to this community
Seen and unseen
We would not be standing here today
And the experience of many public housing residents in this
community, standing on the shoulders of those who came
before them, would never be the same

Asé

ONCE UPON A BLUE MOON

Today is a Sturgeon Moon
A rare Blue Moon

I spent the end of my evening preparing for it
Laying out all of my crystals on the back porch to recharge
Meditating over Yemaya for support with healing and releasing
pent-up trauma from old wounds, dispelling grief, and
protection
Bathing in lavender Epsom salt and Florida Water

Immersing my entire body underwater
Sweating toxins
Guided by candlelight
My spirit reawakened with incense
One for love and knowledge
Another for good fortune

Listening to Sade
Purging through my tears
Calling on the Universe and my ancestors to help facilitate the
clearing of my chakras
Professing who I want to be and subsequently who I no longer
want to be
Exhaling internal harm heavily

Windows open for fresh air
I say a prayer
Affirming myself with asé and amen
Ending the session naked on my bed
The residue of toxins still dripping through my pores
Under a string of soft low lights
Massaging my body with shea butter
Hydrating with a liter of alkaline water

Uranus is officially in retrograde

OUR BLACKNESS IS BEAUTIFUL

Our Blackness is beautiful
Something to be celebrated
The reverse case of a funeral
A place where Black lives have wisdom with more eyes than the
characters of Roman numerals
Let's pour out the libations for the death of our unworthiness
The worldliness and burliness of our oppression prevent us
from somehow living in a world of bliss
We think we're opposites
but we're not
Just spiritual beings on different journeys with similar stories but
different plots
Just curvaceous bodies on similar planes flying through space to
different spots
Just love making creatures tryna feel all of the love that a broken
heart got

Blackness is beautiful
Joyful
Like the noise of four-part choir harmony on Sunday in a Baptist
church
Lit
Like 90s house parties with sweaty backs and vibrating rumps
shaking the Earth
Funny
Like inside jokes and silent innuendos in public with the homies
that have you laughing from the pit of your stomach to the base
of your throat

Blackness is beautiful
And simply abundant
Like
No matter what tomorrow brings, I'm rich in this moment
Abundant like
No matter what your mama got in her bank account, she rich in

the Lord
Like
"Who all at the party?" cause I'm bringing my boys
Abundant like
We got everything we need so come through with the kids
Like
I know I'm in between paychecks but I'm still sharing my ends

Blackness is beautiful
And something to be celebrated
Hot combed pressed down and banquet dressed up elevated
My energy proceeds me
Recurring lifetimes receive me
UniverSoul graded
I stay blessed up
Never faded
No circus in this business
Cause one monkey don't stop no show
You gon always see me smile
Churning from a love within that some will never know
Because I recognize that...

Our Blackness is beautiful
And it's something to be celebrated

PATRIOTISM

I am Black
I am woman
I am a little unorthodox
I am a muthafuckin patriot
Just because I wasn't meant to be

They say a patriot is someone who loves or fights for their
country
Well, my people built this country with their bodies
And shed blood for this land
And I love my people
So I guess that makes me a patriot

This is America
Let me re-envision
Flip it
Reverse it
Throw a little witchery in it
Kick down yo doe to take back what's mine and throw a little
trickery in it
Let this be my America

Star Spangled Banner - The Remix
Oh say can you see, bodies burning through the night
What so proudly we hang, from a flag that stays waving
Whose broad stripes and bright stars, wrapped in violent cause
On the TVs we watch, we're so gallantly bleeding
With capitalism's red glare, Black and brown gains aren't fair
Gave proof through the night, deported friends were not there
O say does that Star-Spangled Banner yet wave
This ain't the land of the free but we're the home of the brave

The Pledge of Allegiance - The Remix (call and response)
I pledge allegiance
To my people

In the US and the Global South
And to challenge the republic
And the foundation on which it stands
In honor
And reverence
Of the many indigenous nations
That founded this nation
With no recognition
Except on occasion
Under God
In a divisible country
We're an indivisible people
With healing
And liberation
And justice
For all

REBIRTH

Time to get moving
Yellow baby butterfly
New life and rebirth
Resurrection
Sometimes you have to cut the cord to heal and find joy

I have been reborn

SEXUAL HEALING

When everything falls away, there is me
Deeply desiring affection
On the regular

The most sacred affection that can be offered to the flesh
Feeling the pulse of touch all over my body
On the regular

Calming every nerve and string of anxiety beaded throughout
my body
Daydreaming I'm showered with kisses
Planted
Everywhere
On the regular

Like a bed of roses
Or dandelions that seem to grow everywhere uncontrollably
Hearing how beautiful I am every waking moment so I find the
energy to be beautiful even when
I'm not feeling beautiful
On the regular

Feeling special
So special that I don't fall prey and melt into the arms of the
men and women who can only temporarily make me feel special
in the moment
Comforted
Ravaged
On the regular

Stroked and choked gently
Softly bitten during penetration
Mildly entertained by the stranger I've become
Roleplay
Missionary bores me

Unless body ministry is included
Exploring every cave and crevice and orifice

Kisses planted
On both sets of lips
Simultaneously
Or one at a time
I enjoy a small tea party
With the delicacy of tongue
Giving me life
On the regular

With each additional breath I take
Each one
More rapidly than the last
The delicacy
Curled in the front
Flat in the back
Like a 90s hairstyle on the cover of Jet

Breasts fondled
Fondling breasts
Length and girth desired
Tribal girth
Godly girth
My little chubby cheeks tapped by the instrument of girth

Making beautiful music
Not for baby making
Just for pleasure
We suppress these things for others
Made to feel ashamed of our own sexual energies
Called selfish for desiring to explore
Especially if others are unwilling or disinterested or unable to
supply

So, we bury them...deep

Where no one can see them
Only we can feel them
When our body tells us what's missing

SOLOGAMY: THE CEREMONY OF SELF

#LetUsBreathe Collective's #BreathingRoom Space
April 1, 2018

This isn't your average ceremony.

And I'm not your average mistress of ceremonies.

This isn't a vow of any kind against men, or women for that matter, meant to make me a sacrificial lamb under the auspice of living single because I'm hurt or broken or confused.

This is a love song.

Meant to be absolutely beautiful.

A sweet harmony of birds chirping to songs in the key of life.

And I wondered why it was made to fit me so perfectly.

This tune has a rhythm that gives you the blues with no lyrics.

And the only snares you can hear is the beat of your heart making love to your chest because that one sound reminds us that we're alive.

Isn't she lovely? I sing to myself.

Grateful that I have a mother who cared enough to stick around when the going got tough and the hood got too rough, picking my chin up and fixing my crown when I couldn't see beyond the soleless/soulless shoes that made me feel like a peasant.

Grateful to my father, who preferred the bottle over crack but couldn't put the bottle down long enough to see the cracks in his mind that left behind a mental illness that goes unchecked so every problem ends at the barrel of a gun or a fist fight.

Being tested and overcoming the fears of death by his hands and absentee tears of abandonment now dried in the sand have contributed to making me who I am.

Thankful for the little girl still trapped inside who reminds me every day that my spirit is only flying to be free.

I clipped her wings way back when I didn't quite know how to be, me.

And now that she's growing them back, I'm making room for her to breathe.

This sologamous ceremony is a commitment to be me.

It's a commitment to myself.

A commitment to be free.

That despite whatever happens from here on out, I've made a commitment to be whole, and in that wholeness a commitment to find reprieve.

And no, I don't believe that anyone can "complete" me.

And I'm not interested in "completing" anyone else, especially when they're not attuned to what it means to be their whole self, completely.

I'm not interested in being possessed or controlled.

I'm pretty sure I know what's best for me.

And yes, this flawless vessel will stay revealed for as long as I feel comfortable in my skin.

And yes, this attitude will continue to check and balance your energy for as long as you choose to enter my presence and speak.

This ceremony is a self-commitment, to live my best life unapologetically, despite who walks through the revolving doors of my heart on this energetic plane, universally.

The rhetoric of my generation is that you're somehow missing out on life if you're not married or don't have children by the age of 30. That you've failed along the way. That you somehow haven't accomplished much until you check those boxes that everyone else is clearly struggling with.

But I commit to not getting lost in time and absorbed by lower frequencies.

I have defeated the odds.

I've beat the statistics of the streets.

I fight for the liberation of Black lives.

Attempting to make sure that all my people eat.

I commit to continue executing my purpose with fidelity, until the day I transition.

I commit to being the epitome of love.

I commit to walking in my truth.

I want everything good and beautiful that life may have to offer.

I commit to myself first so that everything thereafter can be erected on the solid foundation of a self that stands tall.

God, as the essence of the Universe, thank you!

I vow to love who I am.

I vow to begin by loving myself.

I vow to love myself for the ways I have grown.

I vow to love my fierce intelligence, my deep potential. Love the ways I am like no one else.

I vow to love the ways I change my mind.

I vow to love the fact that I am not the same person I used to be. Love the person I am becoming.

I vow to love my future wild mistakes.

I vow to love the tomorrows I am heading into. Love that I will end up doing more than I can ever imagine.

I vow to love it when I'm bold enough to stand alone. Love it when I'm tender enough to need support.

I vow to love my ups and downs, my sudden cravings, my quirks, my hopes for something more.

I vow to love the parts of me that need more loving, and always, even when it is lots of work, love the parts of me that I would prefer to hide.

I vow to not forget that I am full of possibility, to not forget that the world awaits me.

I vow to know I am right where I belong.

I vow to be just the person I need to be.

I vow to love myself gently with my whole heart. Love my

silliness and my seriousness.

I vow to love my complexities, delight in the ways I cannot be defined, and love the ways I cannot be tamed.

I vow to love it when I realize I have learned something, and love it when that learning has been good.

I vow to love myself when things are hard. Love myself even when it hurts.

I vow to love myself enough to give myself the things I need.

I vow to keep loving myself until that love becomes a habit.

I vow to love myself so that the world can see how beautifully I deserve to be treated, and keep on loving myself with joy and perseverance. Right down to the bottom of me, as I love a dear friend.

I vow to love exactly who I am.

SPIRIT GUIDES

Sometimes I hear her, whispering in my ear with the wind of a
hot summer breeze
I have to close my eyes just to listen to what she's saying because
the voice is so faint
Her voice was so verbose when I was a child
I could hear her loud and clearly calling me in from the street
when I was out too late

"The streetlights are warming up. Girl, you betta get your
narrow behind home."
Or when I had myself somewhere where I knew my mother told
me I wasn't supposed to be
"Now, you know you not supposed to be here. You just asking
for trouble."

Her voice rang loudly through the pit of my stomach
It was deep, baritone-like
She smelled of cinnamon tea cakes that warmed her heart but
were far too chewy for her taste
She hated to discipline me
It clearly hurt her much more than it hurt me but we both knew
it had to be done
I would often travel to see her at night
On the weekends
I rode on an astral plane that I didn't even know that I had access
to

She was family, and always would meet me somewhere in the
middle because I was far too young to go too far
Yet far enough to take on a role and responsibilities that no one
ever prepared me for
I started caring for others the way she cared for me
I watched the people I loved get abused
I watched the people who claimed to love the people I love
abuse me

Through it all, she held my hand
Until one day, she let go
Perhaps she felt that I needed my own wings to fly
But I still needed protection
I needed her
I resented her for going away
For abandoning our journey together as I grew
She stopped calling
Stop inviting me on trips to see her
She no longer wanted to play

When I finally had the courage to speak of her, I was told that
she died
A terrible death
Unresolved with curious conviction
It's been a while but I recently decided to return home to pay
my respects and make my peace
Without anger or resentment or disappointment for her not
being able to save me
I talk to her, ya know, aloud
I still hear her speak
Whispering in my ear with the wind of a hot summer breeze
The more I release, the louder her voice becomes...again

Deep, baritone
Like she never left
She was just waiting to be understood

THE ALLITERATION OF FEAR

For every altered road

Fair expenditures are redeemed

Failure, exceptionally, always replays

Fresh echos all resounding

Frankly, errors are required

For every accomplished reward

Feeling egos arising, relishing

Flipping expectations around, reawakening

Forgetting essentials as realizations

Forging equitable assemblages revolving

F.E.A.R.

Means what it means to you. Everything that you want or ever could need is on the other side of that assigned, not fixed, meaning.

Fear

What does it mean to you?

THE CHILDREN OF GRIEF

Grief is hard
Hard like cobblestone pebbles on the bank of a man-made
beach that you've been called to take refuge in exchange for
peace
The surface of which scratches the arches of your feet and
punctures your toes until it's too unbearable to walk through the
water
At which point you either run back to the shore or further into
the water
Only to find yourself suddenly succumbing to the unexpected
drop-off that submerges you completely underwater
As you discover that it was not a beach after all but a lake
With no lifeguards, buoys, or any place to retreat to for reprieve
As your head bobs in and out of the water
Your mouth gasping for air to catch a breath
Your arms flailing back and forth
Exhausting you even more
And just when you feel you don't have any more fight left in you
A stranger rows a lifeboat your way from the shore
Rescuing you from the nearby glory hole of a vortex pulling you
in

Today, in your battle with gravity, you won
Yet every single day is a new battle undefeated
A new battle with no strangers or lifeboats
Just you
And the darkness of your mind
Coupled with the sadness of your heart
It's temporary
But inconsistently constant
Over an extended period of time

Grief is strange like that

They say all things get better with time

I'm still not sure whether that applies here
Grief doesn't get better
It just changes into something different every single time
Our ability to adapt to the constant that is change gets better
As it changes, we change with it
But
We are never beyond grief
We are always grieving
Something
Someone

Our grieving
It remains the same

THE MORNING AFTER...A LESSON ON THE POLITICAL ECONOMY OF CRISIS

January 7, 2021

Context
"Domestic terrorism: Violent, criminal acts committed by individuals and/or groups to further ideological goals stemming from domestic influences, such as those of a political, religious, social, racial, or environmental nature." - FBI.gov

An armed mob of white folks stormed the U.S. Capitol yesterday, an act that hasn't happened since the British occupied the area in 1814, during the War of 1812, and set the place ablaze. A whole attempted coup d'etat. They scaled the walls of the federal building, broke windows and doors, broke into the offices and chamber of our congresspeople, stole things for souvenirs, planted pipe bombs, injured multiple police officers, contributed to the killing of a woman, and put the entire Capitol on lockdown. The insult and disgusting manifestation of white privilege in the name of patriotism and democracy was palpable. But in the words of Malcolm X and other literary pundits that came before and after him, "The chickens have come home to roost".

Reflection
Yesterday, I heard President-Elect Joe Biden mention that what we witnessed yesterday (i.e., the domestic terrorists storming the Capitol) does not represent America when indeed it does. Everything that this nation experienced yesterday is truly the heart and soul of this country. This is the result of a climate of hate aka the chickens have come home to roost. The sooner we acknowledge that, the more effective we'll be in moving forward racial equity work. Every system is designed to benefit itself. The fact that the police state stood by allowing it to happen, somehow not fearing for their lives as they interestingly do with unarmed Black bodies, opening barricades for easy

access, and taking selfies with armed insurgents known to not just be Trump supporters but explicitly anti-black, homophobic, xenophobic, anti-equity and anti-parity sends a strong message that racist white supremacists are no enemy of the state. They are a part of the state. There are exceptions but make no mistakes, white supremacy is the rule, which is why the application of the double standard in this scenario is luminous.

How does this happen in one of the most militarized cities in the nation? A city where there is secret service presence at national monuments and museums. This wasn't the work of a small eager extremist mob. Something of this magnitude and scale could only be hand-crafted this well from the inside and sorry to be the bearer of reality but it's not just Donald Trump going rogue. The erosion of democracy has simply been amplified under his fascist administration. It didn't start here and it won't end here. Van Jones (of CNN) asked the question yesterday, is this the beginning or end of something? It's definitely both but you can bet it's the beginning of something and if you allow yourself to be lullabied to sleep by the propaganda being spent your way, you're gonna regret it. This is not a conspiracy. A conspiracy is a secret plan by a group to do something unlawful or harmful. There was nothing secretive about this. The Proud Boys, QAnon, Oath Keepers, Three Percenters, and others have been explicitly expressing their intentions on public platforms.

Last night, I heard major media outlets say the Capitol Police weren't prepared but this happened in the District of Columbia, the capital of the free world, where there is more law enforcement than Capitol Police. Does this lack of preparation extend to them as well? Beyond the Capitol Police, to say that the folks who specialize in national security and tasked with the protection of our republic weren't prepared for what happened is an absolute lie and grossly negligent. And if this is truly the case, and they actually weren't prepared for a violent armed mob in our nation's capital, why are we allocating resources for these services? If you're not able to protect the republic, how are you able to protect and serve civilians? We're not asking the right questions people, and we're focused on the wrong things at the right time. I saw more factions of aggressive police presence on the streets of Chicago in 2020 for unarmed protestors peacefully marching for Black lives than what I witnessed during an armed insurrection in DC yesterday for hours on end, even after the mayor-imposed curfew. Ops hiding in plain sight. Why they chose not to do anything about it is the question we should really be asking ourselves. How does any of this support the hyperbolic agenda of the state, because it's not just about Trump being a sore loser and delaying the certification of election results.

I'm someone very much concerned with policy with a keen understanding that race is inextricably linked to capitalism. So when in doubt, I always follow the money. There is a movement to defund the police (as they are perpetually being rendered obsolete) and reallocate resources where they are actually needed for survival and community stabilization. What greater way to put the priorities of the police state on the policy agenda than making America feel unsecured/insecure in their own backyard?! If someone breaks into your house, you don't remodel the kitchen as a resolution. You invest in security and surveillance apparatuses. You spend your savings on cameras and a security system as a preventive measure to make you feel comfortable with the fact that although you couldn't have prevented it, you will certainly make sure that it doesn't happen again. To the well-intentioned American who might hear how "unprepared" they were, many of you may throw up your hands and say, well, how do we get them prepared to make sure that this never happens again? To which the state will respond, "So glad you asked. Here's a list of strategic priorities and (re)investments that we'd like to soft bake into the next Education bill."

Stay focused! Don't get distracted by 4K footage from

the inside! Keep fighting for systemic change with the people most impacted the center. What we experienced yesterday was domestic terrorism, sedition, and tyranny. I wouldn't quite classify it as treason because there would have to be an act of betrayal present and well, in my empirical experience as a 30 something year old Black woman in America, I see none here.

THE MOTHERLAND

Whenever I am here, I am forced to confront some part of
myself that I seek to bury
That I seek to leave behind but do not quite know how to use
the tools that I have to build my way out
So I build myself further in, burying my heart and consciousness
with vitriol because I haven't quite mastered how to forgive and
release

Some time has passed yet I'm still burying
Myself
Mourning the tie to my soul
The plot not yet determined how deep

I'm burying
My head first, so I don't have to think about how irrational I feel
for desiring adrenaline
That rushes for hearts made of gold
But mistaken for brass like mine
Disrespected
Forgotten, even brass has been carefully crafted with copper and
zinc

Mama Africa sees me as I am
Not as who I want to be
She loves me
Not for who I'm becoming
But who I've become
When I stop moving long enough to breathe, I cry

My inhales filled with pain
From processing being present in the moment

Kill the noise

Exhales of exhaustion

I've been waiting so long to exhale
Mama Motherland
Is whispering
She wants me to leave my baggage behind on the shores of the
banks where the souls of Black folk cry for us just so we can be
free crossing waters
Unchained
By trauma
My trauma
Though not completely understood, I carry with me

My pain
Trained to navigate, I usher through me
My resentment
Turned
Bitter
Adjective
Feeling or showing anger, hurt, or resentment because of bad
experiences or a sense of unjust treatment

Unjust treatment
Unjust treatment

I am bitter...because of a man that I cannot seem to stop loving,
even though I have tried
I am bitter...because of a man that I cannot seem to stop loving
I am bitter...because of a man.
I am bitter…

Fraught with trauma that weighs heavy on my broken heart
I am a woman
My smile and resolute behavior unmarred by my sadness
Questioning whether these spells are symptoms of depression
or just heartbreak

Unacknowledged
Unnoticed

Misunderstood
How many more years will it take to heal?

Whenever I'm on this continent, I feel close to home
Acknowledgement
Notice
Understanding
In the wind
I'm present

My guard
My shield
My protective coat of armor
It is shed from my being
It is not needed here
At least not in the way that it is needed in the rest of the world
In my birth country of America
I desire to be free

God wrapped her arms around me at Robinson Island in Diani
Nothing to cloud my mind in Kenya
Staring into clear waters
I am pictured as a mirage
My heart and mind forced to contend with that which is
suppressed
With
Noise

Kill the noise

God's waters
Her vessel
Utter appreciation
In the Motherland
Another buried burden released

THE MOURNING

This is where I leave you.

I've been crying for days.

Not because of what you said but because I know that this is where I must leave you.

You called to let me know that you received my graduation invitation.

Instead of saying congratulations or job well done, you decided to let me know how much you disliked my hair or lack thereof; how much you disapproved of my bald head, and how I looked with bald hair.

As if I could care about your opinion of what I perceive to be incredibly beautiful, a work of art in her rawest form.

Never mind the fact that I just received a Ph.D.

Never mind the fact that you're reaching out two days after my birthday and don't even know that I just turned 36, or that I just had a birthday at all.

Never mind the fact that I've had my head shaved bald for the last two years and my sides were shaved six years before that.

Never mind the fact that within those last two years, we started talking again after many years of no contact, and you've seen and taken pictures with me not once but twice with my bald-headed ass, and you've said nothing of the sort to my face.

Never mind the fact that I was just minding my own successful Black business when you called in your drunken stupor, per usual. Slurring your words without a care in the world for the consequences of your verbal lashings.

You told me that you didn't call for conflict but you did, prepared for me to meet your ignorance with belligerence so you can justify another aggressive act of belligerence against me.

You pick fights to make it easier to cope and live with the guilt of who I've become despite all that you are, and certainly all that you are not.

In the midst of your lashing, I discover what this is really about when you scoldingly tell me that I'm a girl, as if I'm unaware; that I'm your daughter and it's not right for me to have my hair this way. You say you want to come to the graduation but you're just not OK with it and you just have to let me know that it's not right.

All this about my sexuality. You've left homophobic voicemail messages about me that you didn't think would get back to me before. Your homophobia irritates me. I wish you would just come out and ask me outright if I'm gay so I can tell you that I'm bisexual and we can be done with it.

I wish you would just come out and ask me outright so I can tell you how the shaving of my hair has nothing to do with who I like to fuck and everything to do with the connection to my divine feminine energy, an energy that took me many years to identify with because I spent a great deal of my life only knowing what it was like to live in the aggressive, masculine, angry energy of the gift that you gave me.

I found myself, fell in love, and loved her deeply; no thanks to you.

Never mind any of that though. You would be perfectly satisfied if all of me were to come undone just for your edification.

Not so you can be there to pick up the pieces but so you can kick me while I'm down, over and over again, because misery loves a good kickback.

And here I am, still taking your calls. Still hearing you out, knowing that you don't have the capacity to make room or space for anything that I have to say while exposing myself to unnecessary harm. Triggering the childhood trauma that I've been working many years to address on my own with no guidance and little resolve.

I'm in mourning because I know that this is where I must leave you.

Without another revolving door for you to come back through and attempt to tear me down again for no reason other than the fact that you can, so you do.

I've been crying, real tears, for days.

Because I know that when you had the audacity and niggerosity to tell me you loved me after disparaging me this week, you actually believed that you did, but the words from your mouth to my ears made me cringe. It felt painful to hear. I didn't believe you. I don't believe you. Moreover, I deserve better than a love that is rooted in pain.

I'm mourning.

And it really hurts.

Yet this is where I leave you.

THE REDWOODS

In the Redwoods
Amidst the Sequoias
In Del Norte County
California
I marvel at some of the largest trees in the world
I show gratitude to my maker
And refuel myself with the breath of life
Purging my lungs of toxins
The air is clearer out here
The gentle moistured mist lay over me
I'm reminded that God is real
Reminded that there is always so much that is bigger than me
Especially that which I do not see
The cool breeze wraps itself within me
I feel holy
Magical
Majestic

The divinity in the Universe recognizes the divinity in me
My larger-than-life personality and spunky character feel right at
home here
In context
Although I am small, I feel big and beautiful
Knowing that in the circle of life, my body alone could help
fertilize The Lost Monarch to the sun
In the Grove of Titans
I pray for recurring peace and restoration
I feel whole again
Nature is my medicine

I ground my bare feet in the backyard of my Airbnb, facing the
woods
Facing the water
The sounds of the Pacific Ocean whistling through the wrestling
trees

I sway along with them
Though they will be here much longer than I
We are both grateful to be alive

THE UNPRAYER

It's so crazy how a man can make a woman question everything about herself, especially when that man is her father

Like the first man who was ever supposed to love me didn't so, how can any man ever love me, really?

I'm not talking about a holy father but a father in need of holy water, a baptism in water holier than the alcoholism that my father, he who is holier than thou, drowns in

I'm not talking about our father who art in heaven but a father who metaphorically lives in the ghetto of the heaven that Tupac wondered about

Hallowed be thy name

Thy kingdom has come from the west side of Detroit

Thy will be done pistol poppin on any mile and Woodward

Or so you thought

It's crazy how one conversation can take you back to that moment when you first started developing that childhood trauma here on Earth, not as it was in heaven before you transitioned into this new karmic space, this new fleshly body that now is simply a receptacle that stores the mental and emotional imprints of all of his abuse

Give us this day, where my joy is his pain and my pain is his love, and he loves to hate me all over

Our daily bread, breaking in pieces of me that crumble every single time I reopen the door for an alter call of his "love"

Still painful, mostly because it's so toxic that I can barely breathe, and the only salvation pulling my spirit up for air is the need is to be saved from him

No matter how many times I forgive his trespasses, I can never seem to forget because he is constantly trespassing against me

Throwing unnecessary daggers

Kicking unnecessary stones

Pouring kerosene on my old but healing wounds and setting them ablaze, leading himself into more temptation

I wish I could deliver us both from evil but it's hard when the devil is your daddy and you're made in his image

It don't take a mirror to see the residue of his destruction reflected back inside of me

These demons I didn't create yet I fight them every day because I know there's a God in me

At least that's what I believe

She shines and grinds and rhymes, and that's how I know for thine is the kingdom, mine is the Queendom, my spiritual vines hold the wisdom so my aura don't have to come to play

But may the power of his will to be better be better tomorrow than what it was today

May the glory of his ego give peace of mind instead of simply a piece of his mind to anyone who will listen…to the hate he spews from the shadows of his darkness

And may I heal without being retriggered over and over again, mistakenly perpetuating and passing down a cycle for another generation to endure, the karmic legacy of which lasts forever and ever more

May this unprayer not go unacknowledged in the world of prayer

May it be heard from the devil's congregation to God's ears

For the unprayer, let the church say, amen

TO KNOW ONE'S HISTORY

To know one's history is a privilege, manifesting as a rite of passage. The ability to rest between the wings of the long-necked heron that we recognize as the visual representation of Sankofa, while she covers us as we look into our pasts to gain a deeper understanding to achieve guidance and wisdom on our journeys to our future, is a superpower from the ancestral gods.

To live, and I do truly mean live, in the present is to transform ourselves beyond the carceral state of our physical bodies. To gift ourselves the luxury of time and treat it as rare and precious as the existential entity that it is. Freedom is having the time to *live*.

To know our history is to appreciate the gifts that our ancestors have bestowed upon us. To lay down the burden of shame. To acknowledge that carrying the gifts that fuel the fire of the torch that we hold is not a burden but a blessing.

To know one's history is to know what you know and know that it doesn't matter what you don't know but how and what you do with what you do know, just because you *know*...better.

WADING

Wade in the water
Wade in the water children
Wade in the water
God's gonna trouble the water

Wade in the water
Wade in the water children
Wade in the water
God's gonna trouble the water

I've been wading
In muddy waters for a long time
Working toward my own self-healing and our collective
liberation
I've been waiting
For my body to readjust from a state of submission
These last several years never got my permission, my consent to
breathe
It was simply on autopilot
Flying under the radar because it was convinced that moving
undetected is what it had to do to be free

I've been waving
But not for the picture they got me posing
Yah say that I'm still chosen
Yet they bowing shooting arrows like
I'm the Bull's eye
But yet we in the city with Benny
He got the Bull eye
But what you don't see that you get
Is from my third eye
Cause I walk by faith and the sight of my sixth chakra
The vibration of my intuition does more dance than a TikToker
Singing Prince's purple rain in the purple reign of my body's aura
My heart the love symbol of things that bring me joy aaaahh

I come in peace

Tell me
How much time do you spend working on your energy?
What do you do to center yourself and stay working on your purpose?
To quiet your mind and stay grounded in Earth's surface?
How you turning your body into a vessel of service?
And showing gratitude for every life lesson emergent?

Who are you looking to for guidance before you jump to conclusions?
Mama (Zora Neale) Hurston had the nerve to walk her own way in search for reality, rather than climb upon the rattling wagon of wishful illusions.

How heavy are the shoulders of the ancestors on which you laugh?
Papa (James) Baldwin taught us that ignorance, allied with power, is the most ferocious enemy justice can have.

What you doing to sharpen the iron that strengthens your mind's needs?
Auntie (Toni) Morrison said we can do some rather extraordinary things if that's what we really believe.

What are you creating with your heart, head, hands, and your feet? What are you sharing that can be gifted to the art of your beat?

Uncle (Amiri) Baraka says warriors are poets and poems and all the loveliness here in the worlds

I bet he's proud of the movement forged from the art of our little BIPOC pearls

He says that art is a weapon in the struggle of ideas

He says art is whatever makes you proud to be human, my dear

And so we
Still fight with every tool we have to get free
As we meddle through the messiness of the things that bind us
As we work to stop throwing stones from the glass houses that
blind us
We are all wading

Wade in the water

I've been reading
All about love
But it feels like there aren't enough hooks for the bells and
whistles that blow within me

Wade in the water children wade in the water

Like Fire
Like Air
Like Earth
Like Water
For chocolate
Bodies cocooning for respite
My girl Ife says the sound of liberation isn't sirens
She asks what does liberation sound and taste like to you?

God's gonna trouble the water

Close your eyes
Take a deep breath
Imagine the greatest feeling you've ever felt
The greatest food you've ever tasted
The greatest scent you've ever smelt
The most pleasant sound you've ever heard
The safest touch you've ever experienced
The first moment you realized that love was a verb

Bottle that euphoria
Flex it into the memory of your muscles
And seal it with rest
You'll need it for your journey
As you continue to be put to the test
While you...

Wade in the water
Wade in the water children
Wade in the water
God's gonna trouble the water

Some of y'all betta be lucky I got my mama's humility
because my daddy's arrogance ain't nothin nice

WE FAMILY

I find that the more I decolonize my body and heal myself from my womb to my crown, the more I am in conflict with my family

The toxic behaviors that I was bred into become more stark
Less digestible
Simply intolerable
Family were fucking with me as long as I went along with their bullshit
A passive participant in my own demise because...hey, "we family"
A phrase in Black families and Black culture that has implied that it doesn't matter what is done to you, no matter how egregious or bad, you should find the will to get over it and move past it for the sake of the family
That ask doesn't quite imply working through it either though because that actually requires everyone being accountable and taking responsibility for their own actions and behaviors

"We family"

A subconscious pass for people to come at you any kinda way
Talk to and treat you disrespectfully and keep moving as if you have no other choice but to accept it
Not listen to one word you have to say when you try to resolve or simply be heard because they felt right and justified in their actions
Sadly, we don't hold space for others' emotions in Black families because no one held space for us

Subsequently, we don't even know how to hold space for ourselves
We just know that we need it
At one point, it was family over everything to me
The ultimate "we family" representative

My 'captain save the family' face ass
My 'can't we all just get along' head ass
Mediating conflict and having sidebar coaching sessions
I thought I was really doing something
As long as everyone went home happy
As long as I could make you laugh, we were good
Call me the non-credentialed family therapist of the ghetto
You couldn't tell me nothing about nobody that bore the legacy
of my maternal grandfather and grandmother's name

For years, I extended myself deep
Showing up for every gathering
Gifting my last at every birthday and holiday
Tap dancing for love
Paying for affection
Knowing that I was seeing and experiencing problematic ass
behaviors concerning abuse and violence and rage but I
rationalized it away with understanding and justifications
Embodying and perpetuating the toxicity that I didn't even
know I needed to disrupt, I just knew it felt good
Like a time-bound temporary high
Until it came down
And reality set in
Over a period of many years

The reality that the same people I bent over backward for
wouldn't do it for me
The reality that the same people I spent my last going broke for
ain't have a dollar or word of encouragement for me when I was
down bad
The reality that I could get it too if a mog felt savage enough
The reality that I couldn't actually save anyone but myself and
when I started to save myself, I realized that all of us were
drowning
Flailing hands in the air with only our eyes above water

I've been away

Working on myself
Disrupting
Healing
Purging the harm I've learned, reinforced through culture

I've been away
Securing my oxygen mask first before trying to help others
secure theirs as we all brace for impact
I've been finding peace
In self-preservation
And happiness
In gratitude
Shedding away my need to take comfort in subjecting myself to
psychological, emotional, and spiritual harm
Writing away my internal proclivity for constant suffering in
exchange for relationship
Enduring suffering while constantly made to feel punished for
pursuing my purpose
Unfairly critiqued for accomplishing what was destined for me
simply because it's more than what others have done before me
This street code of loyalty gets tough when you're dealing with
hatin ass niggas in your family

"We family" though, right?

Though kinfolk
Not bound by ties of love, but fear

But not at the expense of my sanity
And not for the price of my peace
As James Baldwin in The Fire Next Time said "Love takes off
the masks that we fear we cannot live without and know we
cannot live within."
Love is a state of being
Love doesn't have to look how we were taught that it should be
It can be whatever makes us feel whole, healthy, and complete

WHO WILL CRY FOR THE LITTLE GIRL?

Who will cry for the little girl?
The one who thought that it was the abandonment, alcoholism, and abuse that she endured from her daddy that held her back from healing when it was really the perpetual psychological triggering of her unhealed mother's mothering who was there the whole time.

Who will cry for the little girl?
When no matter how many times she is dismissed, disregarded, dejected, denied, and demonstrated to be of little and insignificant value, she keeps running back into the bosom of the first woman who was ever supposed to love her deep
...hold her close
...squeeze her tight

Who will cry for the little girl?
When she has spent a lifetime prioritizing and protecting people who don't cover or consider her; her sense of loyalty all fucked up from the inside out.

Who will cry for the little girl?
Who was never told that it wasn't her fault that she was molested/raped multiple times by multiple people under her mother's roof before the age of 10 but instead was told that she wasn't believed when only one of many incidents was ultimately revealed.

Who will cry for the little girl?
Who has never known what it feels like to live in safety.

Mentally.
Emotionally.
Physically.

Who will cry for the little girl?

Who continues to spend a lifetime fighting demons because chaos is all she's ever known.

Who will cry for the little girl?
Who always has to stay three steps ahead because she's always getting kicked two steps back.

Who will cry for the little girl?
Who is self-motivated to heal herself despite the sources of her trauma not being motivated enough by the chances of a better relationship with her to heal themselves.

Who will cry for the little girl?
When generational curses have been broken and karmic debt has been paid, and there's no one left standing beside her because of their unwillingness to do the work of overcoming themselves.

Who will cry for the little girl, who even cried for the little boy inside Antwone Fisher years before crying for herself?

Who will cry for the little girl?
Who has nearly run out of tears so instead temporarily dwells in the numbing place until she can feel whole again. Though bleak, it is her own little raisin in the sun. A place to hope. A place to persevere. A place to be free.

Who will cry for the little girl, who dares to be brave yet still cries inside of me?

WINNING BATTLE

I'm fighting for my life and very few people know

Angels bursting from the seams of my soul, dancing with the stars

Battling demons daily, perpetually trying to overcome myself

The cumulative effect of many years of trying to be the bigger person, the perfect human, standing in the strength of the sun, taking it all in like one big receptacle

Binging on the weight of the world, no real place to release the purge

Getting consistently knocked down, around, and upside down but getting back up and coming back ready for more

It's catching up to me

I am resilient
I am enough
And today, I choose joy
Today, I choose to live

Today, I chose life

"You are the Chair and CEO of your own life."
— Melody Spann Cooper, Midway Broadcasting Corporation

Take charge!

GLENANCE AKA DR. G

Glenance Green, Ph.D., affectionately known as Dr. G, is a Chicago writer, researcher, community organizer, and filmmaker who uses various art forms and grassroots strategies as tools of healing and liberation. Glenance is the author of *Shades of Green*, an anthology of poetry and prose, and has written, directed, and/or produced over 10 short films. Dr. G is deeply committed to racial equity and enhancing the quality of life, especially for Black communities. She is the Co-Founder and Executive Director of the Black Researchers Collective, a capacity-building collective of Black researchers on the South Side of Chicago equipping communities with research tools to be more civically engaged and policy informed. Dr. G is a proud resident of Bronzeville, Chicago's historic Black Metropolis, and the Co-Host of *Research in the Streets*, a podcast intended to provide a forum to discuss how research and data can be used by everyday people in everyday life.

For Glenance, every moment in life either presents an opportunity for gratitude, a lesson to be learned, or spiritual alignment with the divine as the essence of the Universe. To revel in appreciation of all three is to bask in our highest good.